Objective tests in economics

Third edition

G F Stanlake

MA BSc(Econ)

may be reproduced, stored in a retrieval system,
or transmitted in any form or by any means, electronic,
mechanical, photocopying, recording or otherwise,
without the prior written permission of the Publishers.

First published 1972
Second edition 1976
Third edition 1988
ISBN 0-582-35444-x

Printed in Singapore by
Huntsmen Offset Printing Pte Ltd

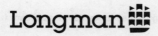

By the same author

First Economics
First Economics Answer Book
Introductory Economics
Introductory Economics Workbook
Macro-economics: an introduction

Longman Group Limited
Longman House

*Burnt Mill, Harlow, Essex CM20 2JE, England
and Associated Companies throughout the World.*

*First published 1969
Second edition 1974
Third edition 1983
ISBN 0 582 35444 7*

Printed in Singapore by
Huntsmen Offset Printing Pte Ltd.

We are grateful to the following for permission to reproduce the photographs on the
cover:
Press Association (left); Topix (centre); Dienst van Gemeentewerken, Rotterdam (right).

Contents

Preface

Multiple choice questions provide a valuable supplement to the well-tried and long-established methods of examining and testing and there is no doubt that much of the subject matter of Economics is very suitable for testing by this method.

The multiple choice type of examination, by making use of a large ? number of questions, can provide a much more complete coverage of the syllabus and, at the same time, presents a limited marking burden. An additional advantage is that the marking itself is objective.

Multiple choice questions can be used for a variety of purposes, but I hope that this book will have three main functions.

1 To aid the student's understanding.
2 To improve the quality of instruction as the tests reveal misconceptions and areas of ignorance.
3 To provide the student with practice in answering this type of question.

The questions are designed to measure different abilities. Very briefly, these abilities may be classified as:

1 *Recall/knowledge:* the ability to recall facts, laws and theories; straight-forward computations etc.
2 *Comprehension:* the ability to translate data from one form to another; to interpret graphs and symbols; to make estimates based on trends in data; to solve problems.
3 *Application:* the ability to apply knowledge, experience and skills to new situations, and to deal with problems presented in an unfamiliar context.
4 *Analysis/evaluation:* the ability to identify a conclusion made from statements; to analyse information and to make judgements.

All the questions in this book are based on material that is commonly taught in A-level courses.

Note on the Third Edition

The changes in this edition are relatively minor. Some 20 questions have been revised or substituted in order to update the subject matter being tested.

Structure of objective questions

An objective test is made up of a series of questions each of which has only one predetermined correct answer. These questions, or *items* (as they are commonly called) may be of several types, but the most common is the multiple choice item. A multiple choice question consists of two parts,

(a) a *stem* which poses the questions;
(b) a number of *responses* or *options,* only one of which provides the correct answer. The incorrect responses are known as *distractors.*

The stem may take the form of a direct question or an incomplete statement. The question asked may be based on a diagram, a cartoon, a photograph, statistical data, or a quotation from published material.

There is no hard and fast rule regarding the number of responses in a multiple choice item. Some examining boards have decided that all questions should have five responses while others have opted for four responses. In view of this variation in examining practice, I have included questions with only four responses (lettered A to D). The majority of the questions, however, have five responses (lettered A to E).

Although all the questions in this book are of the multiple choice type, there are several different formats for this type of question. The variety in this book is restricted to the four most common types: Simple completion, Multiple completion, Classification sets, and Assertion—Reason questions. Examples of each type, together with the standard instructions for dealing with them are given below.

Simple completion

This is the basic type of multiple choice question and the instructions for dealing with it are very easy to follow.

Each of these questions is followed by five (or four) suggested answers.
   Select the best answer in each case.

   Example   The terms of trade refer to a relationship between
                A the total volumes of exports and imports
                B the total values of exports and imports
                C the relative prices of exports and imports
                D the visible trade balance and the invisible trade balance

Multiple completion

This is a more complex type of item where the responses are grouped together in different combinations. The instructions for dealing with these items are as follows:

For each of these questions, ONE or MORE of the responses are correct. Decide which of the responses is (are) correct and then choose one of the combinations lettered A to D (or E).

Example Which of the following would a UK bank regard as liquid assets?

1 Treasury Bills
2 Notes and coin
3 Advances

A 1, 2 and 3
B 1 and 2 only
C 2 and 3 only
D 1 only
E 3 only

Classification sets

In this type of question there are a series of questions all based on the same data. The standard instructions for classification sets are as follows:

Each group of questions consists of five (or four) lettered headings followed by a list of numbered questions. For each numbered question select the heading which you consider to be most closely related to it. Note that each heading may be used once, more than once, or not at all.

Example **Questions 3, 4 and 5** refer to the following headings which are all used in the UK balance of payments:

A Visible trade
B Invisible trade
C Official financing
D Investment and other capital flows
E Balancing item

Under which heading will the following transaction appear?

3 The local services consumed by British troops stationed abroad
4 The export of cars from the American-owned Ford factory at Dagenham
5 The allocation of a balance of payments surplus to the gold and foreign reserves

Assertion—Reason

In this type of question one is asked to evaluate the truth or falsity of two statements and to decide the nature of the relationship between them. The instructions are as follows:

Each of these questions consists of a statement in the left-hand column (the Assertion), followed by a second statement in the right-hand column (the Reason). Select

A if both statements are true and the second statement is a correct explanation of the first statement

B if both statements are true, but the second statement is NOT a correct explanation of the first statement

C if the first statement is true but the second statement is false

D if the first statement is false but the second statement is true

E if both statements are false

Example

First statement

Inflation may be caused by increases in wage rates.

Second statement

An increase in wage rates will increase average costs and hence cause prices to rise.

Answers to examples: 1, C; 2, B; 3, B; 4, A; 5, C; 6, C.

1 Introductory ideas

Scarcity and choice
Opportunity costs
The price mechanism

1 'Economic goods are scarce goods.'

The meaning of the word 'scarce' in this quotation is that

A there are very few of these goods
B there are insufficient goods to meet effective demand
C the goods are limited in supply
D there are not enough of the goods to meet all our wants to the point of satiety
E the goods are insufficient to meet all our physical *needs*

2 Which is the most satisfactory definition of opportunity cost?

A The price of the commodity
B The minimum average cost of production
C The sacrifice of any alternative choice
D The loss suffered by missing some bargain
E The sacrifice of the next most desired alternative

3 Wealth, as the term is used in economics, means

A the total savings of the whole community
B the stock of capital goods valued at the current prices
C total current incomes plus total savings
D the stock of all those goods which have a money value
E the total supply of money (i.e. coins, banknotes and bank deposits)

4 'Substitution, or the sacrifice of alternatives, is the law of life in a full employment economy.'

The idea the writer has in mind is that

A all goods have an elastic demand
B it is always possible to substitute one factor of production for another
C under the conditions specified, every economic good has an opportunity cost
D all capital goods wear out in the long run and can then be replaced by different types
E there are different ways of producing any given commodity

5 The question relates to the following diagram which shows the production possibility curve of a community:

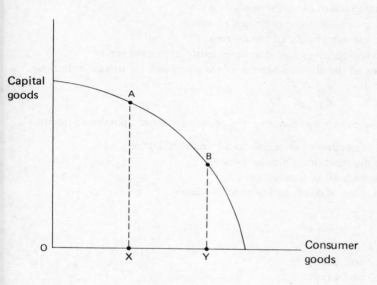

The points A and B represent

A the community's demand for capital goods (i.e. AX) and consumer goods (i.e. OY)

B the maximum possible output of capital goods (AX) and consumer goods (OY)

C possible alternative combinations of capital goods and consumer goods which the community can produce

D a full employment output (A) and a less than full employment output (B)

E none of the above since these alternatives cannot be demonstrated with a production possibility diagram

6   In private enterprise societies, the basic economic problem of 'What goods shall be produced' is decided by

A   making use of extensive specialisation
B   using large amounts of capital equipment
C   the spending habits of the citizens
D   the entrepreneur acting independently of market forces
E   none of the above, since this is not a problem for private enterprise societies

7   In a free enterprise economy, the price mechanism operates to determine

1   the allocation of resources to different industries
2   the distribution of money incomes
3   the methods of production
4   the range of goods and services produced

A   1, 2 and 3 only
B   1, 2, 3 and 4
C   1, 3 and 4 only
D   2 and 3 only
E   2 and 4 only

Questions 8–10 refer to the following statements:

1   Resources are allocated to different uses by means of official permits and licences.
2   Prices fully reflect relative scarcities.
3   The proportions in which land and labour are combined is largely dependent upon the size of the farmer's family.
4   Competition ensures that low cost methods replace high cost methods.
5   Money prices are determined by social priorities. Shortages, then, are revealed by the existence of waiting lists.

8   Which of these statements refer to conditions in a **market** economy?

A   1 and 2 only
B   1, 3 and 5 only
C   2 and 4 only
D   2, 3 and 5 only
E   4 only

9 Which refer to conditions in a **command** economy?

    A 1 and 4 only
    B 1 and 5 only
    C 2 and 3 only
    D 2 and 5 only
    E 3 and 4 only

10 Which refer to conditions in a **traditional** society?

    A 2 only
    B 2 and 3 only
    C 3 only
    D 3, 4 and 5 only
    E 4 only

Assertion—Reason questions

Key	First statement	Second statement
A	True	True, and correct explanation of first statement
B	True	True, but *not* a correct explanation of first statement
C	True	False
D	False	True
E	False	False

11 The job of the economist is to decide on the best way to use the limited supply of economic resources.

By reason of his training the economist is more qualified than the layman to pronounce on how people should satisfy their material wants.

12 The nation's supply of money is part of the national wealth.

Money represents a claim to goods and services.

13 The basic economic problems facing a society will differ according to the type of economic system in use.

Some societies allow market forces to determine the level and pattern of output, while others control the economy by centralised planning.

14 Economics is concerned with the problem of how to use scarce resources which have alternative uses.

Economic goods are scarce because a few people have much more than they want while others have far less than they want.

2 Population

Questions 15 and 16 are based on the following population characteristics:

1 A high birth rate
2 A low average age
3 A high death rate
4 A high expectancy of life
5 A large proportion of over-age dependents
6 A large proportion of young dependents

For the purposes of these questions the following classification should be used:

Young dependents   0–14 years
Working-age groups   15–64 years
Over-age dependents   65+ years

15 Which of the population features would you expect to find in an advanced industrialised Western European country?

A 2 and 6 only
B 4 and 5 only
C 1, 3 and 6 only
D 1, 4 and 6 only
E 2, 3 and 6 only

16 Which of the features would you expect to find in the population of a developing country in Latin America?

A 1 and 3 only
B 1, 2 and 3 only
C 1, 3 and 6 only
D 1, 2, 3 and 6 only
E 1, 3, 5 and 6 only

17 Which was the most significant factor in the rapid increase of British population during the nineteenth century?

A Rising birth rate
B Large-scale immigration
C Falling death rate
D Birth rate rising faster than the death rate
E Restrictions on emigration

Questions 18—21 are based on the following diagram which shows the variations in output as population increases, other things remaining equal:

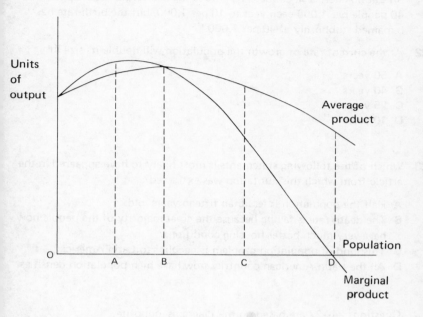

A Size of population OA
B Size of population OB
C Size of population OC
D Size of population OD
E Cannot be determined from the information given

Which of the above describe the following situations?

18 There are increasing returns to labour
19 Population is at its optimum size
20 There are increasing returns to scale
21 Total output is at a maximum

Questions 22 and 23 are based on the following quotation from a recent article on world population:

'In Latin America since the early 1900s the death-rate has dropped from 40 people per 1,000 each year to 10 per 1,000, but the birth-rate has remained stubbornly at 40 per 1,000.'

22 At the current rate of growth the population will double its size in

A 50 years
B 40 years
C 25 years
D 10 years

23 Which of the following statements is most likely to have appeared in the article from which this quotation was extracted?

A Half the population is less than fifteen years old.
B The death rate is falling because the great majority of the people now have very much better housing conditions.
C This kind of population problem is peculiar to Latin America.
D All the Latin American countries now have high population densities.

Questions 24—27 are based on the diagrams opposite.

The diagrams illustrate the age distributions of various populations. Which **shape** is most likely to represent the population of each of the following?

24 A developing country in Latin America
25 A developed industrialised country in Western Europe
26 A residential coastal town in the United Kingdom (e.g. Bournemouth)
27 A recently established and rapidly expanding New Town

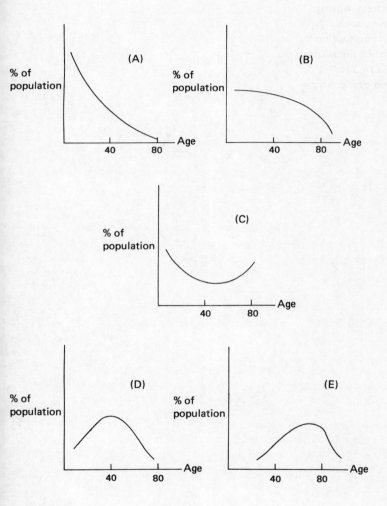

3 Production

28 'When a firm with given capacity is increasing output by taking on more men, there will come a point where the average returns to labour will start to diminish.'

This means that

A total output will start to fall
B the marginal productivity of the other factors will be decreasing
C if wages are constant, labour costs per unit of output will be increasing
D output has expanded beyond the most profitable position
E total revenue will be falling

29 For any given output, the least cost combination of factors is found where

A the marginal products of the different factors of production are equal
B the marginal products of the factors are proportional to their prices
C the law of diminishing returns begins to operate
D the average products of the factors are equal
E the amounts spent on each factor are equal

Questions 30–32 are based on the following table, which shows the ranges of output obtainable with different combinations of the factors of production labour and capital:

		1	2	3	4	5
	5	240	310	370	410	430
Units of	4	220	300	350	390	410
labour	3	190	270	320	350	370
	2	150	220	270	300	310
	1	100	150	190	220	240

Units of capital

30 The data in the table illustrate

A constant returns to labour
B diminishing returns
C diminishing utility
D inelastic supply
E falling costs

17

31 If labour costs £1 per unit and capital costs £3 per unit, which of the following items represents the lowest cost of producing 220 units?

- A £5
- B £7
- C £8
- D £10
- E £13

32 If there were **constant returns to scale** throughout, the amount of output that could be produced with 3 units of labour and 6 units of capital would be

- A 400
- B 410
- C 440
- D 450
- E 590

Questions 33–36 relate to the following economies of scale:

- A Economies of increased dimensions
- B Financial economies
- C Risk-bearing economies
- D Indivisibility of factors of production
- E The principle of massed reserves

To which of the above types do the following examples belong?

33 The large cranes used on large building projects

34 A motor manufacturer making use of very large fully automatic hydraulic presses

35 A large firm manufacturing a wide variety of products

36 A 500,000-ton oil tanker

Questions 37–40 are based on the following diagram which shows the changes in total output as more men are combined with a fixed amount of land and capital:

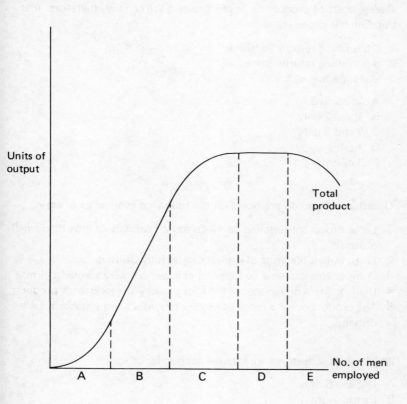

In what ranges of output do we find the following returns?

37 Constant returns to labour

38 Diminishing returns to labour

39 Increasing returns to labour

40 Zero returns to labour

41 A firm acquires more land, extends its factory, installs more machinery, and employs more labour, but it does not change its techniques of production. It then finds that, although factor prices have not risen, its average costs of production have increased. We can say, therefore, that this firm has experienced

1 diminishing returns to labour
2 diminishing returns to capital
3 diseconomies of scale

    A 1, 2 and 3
    B 1 and 2 only
    C 2 and 3 only
    D 1 only
    E 3 only

Questions 42 and 43 are based on the following economies of scale:

1 Large orders are supplied on much more favourable terms than small orders.
2 Large indivisible units of capital can be fully utilised.
3 Components can now be supplied at lower costs by specialist firms.
4 Haulage firms design special vehicles to carry the industry's products.
5 The production of a range of models provides a more stable total demand.

42 Which of these features are **internal** economies of scale?

    A 1, 2 and 5 only
    B 1 and 2 only
    C 2 and 5 only
    D 3 and 4 only
    E 1, 3 and 5 only

43 Which of them are **external** economies of scale?

    A 1, 2 and 5 only
    B 1 and 2 only
    C 1, 3 and 5 only
    D 2 and 5 only
    E 3 and 4 only

Questions 44—46 refer to the following diagram which shows the short-run cost curves of the individual firm:

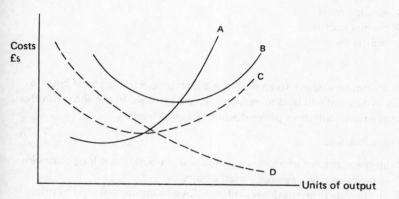

Which of the curves represents

44 Average total cost

45 Average variable cost

46 Average fixed cost

47 The question is based on the following hypothetical data:

In a given industry, wage rates are increased from 200p per hour to 240p per hour; output per man-hour increases by 10%; the number of hours worked decreases from 40 hours to 38 hours per week, and raw material costs rise by 10%.

In the light of these changes which of the following statements is correct?

A Total output rises and labour costs per unit fall.
B Total output rises and labour costs per unit rise.
C Total output falls and labour costs per unit fall.
D Total output falls and labour costs per unit rise.
E Total output rises but labour costs per unit are unchanged.

48 In the short run the total revenue of the firm must cover

    A total costs
    B fixed costs
    C variable costs
    D normal profits
    E capital costs

49 In an industry where fixed costs are a high proportion of total costs, a fall in demand will lead to very severe competition. In the short run this competition will drive prices down to ruinous levels.

This is because

1 in the short run producers will continue in business as long as prices more than cover average variable costs
2 in the short run producers will continue in business as long as prices more than cover average fixed costs
3 average variable costs will be a small proportion of average total costs
4 producers will continue to operate only so long as revenue covers total costs (i.e. fixed plus variable costs)

Which of the above statements are **incorrect**?

    A 1 and 2 only
    B 1 and 3 only
    C 2 and 3 only
    D 2 and 4 only
    E 3 and 4 only

50 The question is based on the following diagram which shows the total cost curve of an individual firm:

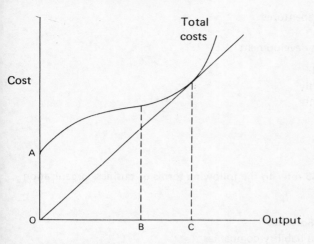

Which of the following statements are correct?

1 OA represents the fixed costs.
2 At an output OB, average costs will be at a minimum.
3 At an output OC, average costs = marginal costs.
4 Over the range of output O to B, average costs will be rising.

    A 1 and 2 only
    B 1 and 3 only
    C 1, 2 and 3 only
    D 1, 2 and 4 only
    E 2, 3 and 4 only

51 'One of the greatest risks in modern industries is that of obsolescence.

Which of the following statements do you consider to be the most realistic explanation of the quotation?

    A Inferior machines wearing out too quickly
    B Unforeseen heavy maintenance costs
    C A rapid rate of technological progress
    D Inflation causing the cost of replacements to rise
    E Continuous operation of machines on a shift-work basis, shortening the life of the machines.

52 Which of the following expenditures are generally classified as Fixed Costs?

1 Interest on debentures
2 Depreciation
3 Research and development

    A 1, 2 and 3
    B 1 and 2 only
    C 2 and 3 only
    D 1 only
    E 3 only

Questions 53—56 refer to the following forms of business organisation

    A Cooperative Societies
    B Public limited liability companies
    C Private limited liability companies
    D Partnerships
    E Public corporations

Which of these institutions have the following features?

53 The dividend paid to the shareholder is not related to the number of share he owns.

54 Shares are freely transferable.

55 The number of members is strictly limited and at least one member must accept unlimited liability.

56 The managers are not elected by the owners; they are appointed.

Questions 57—60 are based on various aspects of business finance:

A A negotiable security which carries the right to a fixed amount of interest which must be paid whether the concern is making a profit or not

B A security which gives a prior claim on profits up to a specified amount, with some share in the remainder

C A security which gives a full claim to residual profits and carries the right to vote at shareholders' meetings

D An agreement between buyer and seller whereby the seller agrees to supply goods in advance of payment

E A short-term marketable security, in the form of an order to pay a fixed sum of money at a specified future date, which has been accepted by the person so ordered

Which of these is known as:

57 A participating preference share

58 An ordinary share

59 Trade credit

60 A debenture

Questions 61—64 refer to the following financial features:

A The purchase of existing shares

B Increasing the stock of machinery in the motor-car industry

C A bank loan for the purpose of buying seeds

D An estimate of the loss in value of the firm's existing assets during the course of a year

E An increase in the value of raw materials and finished goods due to inflationary conditions

Which of the above provides an example of

61 Stock appreciation?

62 Net investment?

63 Depreciation?

64 Working capital?

65 'Limited liability' means

A the number of shares in the company is strictly limited
B all shareholders have the same liability for the company's debts
C the shareholder is only liable for the debts of the company to the extent of the unpaid value of his shares
D all shareholders, except ordinary shareholders, enjoy limited liability
E the company can only incur debts up to some specified amount

Questions 66—68 are based on the following details concerning the financial structure of Company X:

Capital of Company X

100,000 5% Preference shares of £1 each
 50,000 5% Debentures of £1 each
200,000   Ordinary shares of £1 each

After meeting all trading expenses, taxation, and allocations to reserves, the company has £27,500 available for distribution.

66 What rate of dividend will be paid to ordinary shareholders?

A 2½%
B 7¾%
C 9%
D 10%
E 13¾%

67 If the ordinary shares are quoted at £1.60 each what is the current yield?

A 1³/₅%
B 3⅛%
C 6¼%
D 12½%
E 25%

68 The nominal value of the equity of this company is

A £150,000
B £200,000
C £240,000
D £250,000
E £300,000

Questions 69—70 are based on the following measures which are used by the government to influence industrial location:

A Industrial development certificates
B Exemption from payments of local authority rates
C Generous investment grants
D Grants to cover the costs of training local labour
E Provision of government-built factories at very favourable rents

69 Which of these measures would be particularly attractive to a capital-intensive firm?

70 Which of the measures does not make use of the market mechanism?

71 Which of the following is NOT a feature of the Stock Exchange?

A Provides a market in existing shares
B Provides a market in government securities
C Allows dealing only in the shares of those companies which have satisfied certain requirements of the S.E. Council
D Is an important source of finance for new companies
E Dealings are restricted to members of the Stock Exchange

Questions 72 and 73 relate to the following motives for integration:

1 To obtain a greater degree of control over the quantities and qualities of the firm's material inputs
2 To ensure that the firm has an adequate number of retail outlets
3 To widen the range of the firm's products
4 To reduce the extent of competition in the firm's existing markets

72 Which of the above are motives for *vertical* integration?

A 1 and 2
B 1 and 3
C 2 and 3
D 2 and 4
E 3 and 4

73 Which are motives for *horizontal* integration?

A 1 and 2
B 1 and 3
C 2 and 3
D 2 and 4
E 3 and 4

Assertion—Reason questions

Key	First statement	Second statement
A	True	True, and correct explanation of first statement
B	True	True, but *not* a correct explanation of first statement
C	True	False
D	False	True
E	False	False

74	Specialisation makes man perilously dependent on the mechanism of exchange.	Specialisation creates interdependent economic units.
75	Were it not for the Law of Diminishing Returns, the world's food supply could be grown on one acre of land.	The Law of D.R. says that as more and more resources are applied to a given plot of land, there will come a point where the total product starts to diminish.

76 An increase in its fixed costs must raise the firm's marginal cost curve.

Marginal cost indicates the rate at which total costs are increasing (or decreasing).

77 The Stock Exchange is a very imperfect market since the numbers of buyers and sellers is very restricted.

Only brokers and jobbers who are members can trade on the Stock Exchange and membership is strictly limited.

4 Supply and demand

The theory of price determination

78 Which is the most likely **cause** of the increase in price illustrated in the diagram?

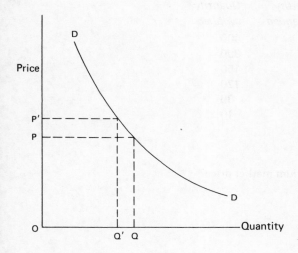

A An increase in consumers' income
B An increase in supply
C An increase in the price of a substitute
D A fall in supply
E A successful advertising campaign

79 There is a relationship between the demands for (and or) the supplies of two commodities (A and B), which are produced and sold in competitive markets. When the production costs of Commodity A are reduced, the demand for Commodity B falls.

Which of the following relationships is most appropriate to the situation outlined above?

A Joint supply
B Competitive demand
C Complementary demand
D Composite demand
E Competitive supply

Questions 80–84 are based on the following demand and supply schedules for Commodity X (units per week):

Price	Quantity demanded	Quantity supplied
50p	100	400
45p	120	300
40p	150	150
35p	200	120
30p	300	80
25p	350	40

80 What is the equilibrium market price?

A 50p
B 45p
C 40p
D 35p
E 30p

81 Demand is inelastic in the range

A 50p–45p
B 45p–40p
C 40p–35p
D 35p–30p
E 30p–25p

82 If a tax of 10p per unit is placed on Commodity X, the new market price will be

A 50p
B 45p
C 40p
D 35p
E 30p

32

83 If the government grants a subsidy of 15p per unit to the producers of Commodity X, the new market price will be

    A 45p
    B 40p
    C 35p
    D 30p
    E 25p

84 In the original situation, if the government fixes a statutory maximum price of 35p

    A consumers will be able to obtain all their requirements more cheaply
    B producers will have a surplus of 80 units per week left on their hands
    C suppliers would produce more
    D some willing buyers will not obtain supplies
    E the demand curve will shift to the right

85 The question is based on the following diagram which shows a change in the conditions of supply, the supply curve moving from SS to S¹S¹:

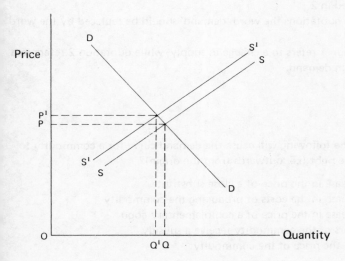

A possible explanation of the movement shown above would be

A a bumper harvest
B a fall in the costs of production
C the granting of a subsidy to producers
D the imposition of a tax on the commodity
E the government declares a statutory price of OP^1

86 The following quotations refer to market situations with downward-sloping demand curves:

1 'If price rises, demand falls.'
2 'If demand rises, price rises.'

Which of the following statements provides the most correct interpretation?

A The quotations are contradictory.
B Quotation 1 is correct, but quotation 2 is incorrect unless we substitute 'quantity demanded' for 'demand'.
C Both quotations are correct, but they are in the wrong sequence. Quotation 1 refers to events which automatically follow those described in 2.
D In both quotations the word 'demand' should be replaced by the word 'supply'.
E Quotation 1 refers to a change in supply, while quotation 2 refers to a change in demand.

87 Which of the following will cause the demand curve for a commodity to move to the right (i.e. outwards from the origin)?

A An increase in the price of a close substitute
B An increase in the costs of producing the commodity
C An increase in the price of a complementary good
D Producers of the commodity receive a subsidy
E A fall in the price of the commodity

88 Commodity X has a close substitute. Assuming a fall in the supply of X, say which of the following changes is likely to occur in the market for the substitute

   A demand will increase and price will increase
   B demand will fall and price will fall
   C price will fall and demand will increase
   D supply will increase and price will fall
   E there will be no change

Questions 89–93 are based on the following diagram:

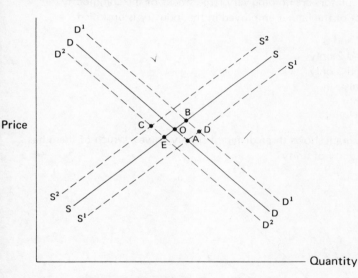

Price

Quantity

O represents an initial equilibrium.

D^1D^1, D^2D^2, S^1S^1 and S^2S^2 represent possible changes in supply and demand.

Which of the letters A to E indicate new equilibrium situations under the new conditions specified below? Assume no change in other conditions.

Product	New conditions
89 Ball-point pens	An increase in productivity
90 Wool	An increase in the demand for mutton

91 'Pop' records   A large fall in the price of tape-recorders

92 Beer   Increased excise duty and an increased preference for wine

93 Fish   A large subsidy to producers and an intensive advertising campaign

94 Which of the following would tend to make the short-run supply of a commodity relatively elastic?

  1 Several firms in the industry are operating with excess capacity
  2 Speculators are holding very large stocks of the commodity
  3 Most of the labour employed in the industry is unskilled

  A 1, 2 and 3
  B 1 and 2 only
  C 2 and 3 only
  D 1 only
  E 3 only

95 The diagram shows three different supply curves. Which of them has an elasticity of unity?

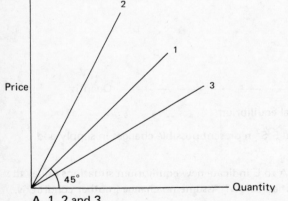

  A 1, 2 and 3
  B 1 and 2 only
  C 2 and 3 only
  D 1 only
  E 3 only

Questions 96—98 relate to the following diagram which shows various possibilities resulting from an increase in demand.

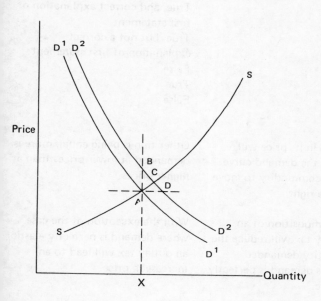

Output is initially at OX.

Which of the points A to D indicate the following?

96 The very short run or momentary equilibrium when there are no reserve stocks

97 The momentary equilibrium when suppliers have adequate stocks to meet an increase in demand

98 The short-run equilibrium established after suppliers have responded to an increase in demand by working their existing resources more intensively

Assertion—Reason questions

Key	First statement	Second statement
A	True	True, and correct explanation of first statement
B	True	True, but **not** a correct explanation of first statement
C	True	False
D	False	True
E	False	False

99   A fall in its price will cause the demand curve for a commodity to move to the right.   Other things being equal, more is demanded at lower prices than at higher prices.

100   The imposition of an outlay tax will reduce the quantity demanded — unless demand is perfectly elastic.   With the exception of the case where demand is perfectly elastic, an outlay tax will lead to an increase in price.

101   If the government offers producers a guaranteed price which is higher than the free market price, there will be a market surplus   At prices higher than the equilibrium market price the quantities supplied will exceed the quantities demanded.

102   The granting of a subsidy to producers will normally lead to an increase in the quantity demanded.   When the demand curve moves to the right more is demanded at each and every price.

5 Market situations

Prices and outputs under:
Perfect competition
Imperfect competition
Monopoly

Questions 103–105 are based on the following data which relate to an individual firm:

Sales (units per week)	Total revenue (£s)
10	100
20	180
30	240
40	280
50	300
60	300
70	280

Fixed costs are £100 per week.
Variable costs are constant at £3 per unit.

103 Demand is inelastic in the price range

A £9–£8
B £8–£7
C £7–£6
D £6–£5
E £5–£4

104 Elasticity of demand is unity in the price range

A £9–£8
B £8–£7
C £7–£6
D £6–£5
E £5–£4

105 The most profitable output for this firm is

A 20 units per week
B 30 units per week
C 40 units per week
D 50 units per week
E 60 units per week

106 The question is based on the following diagram:

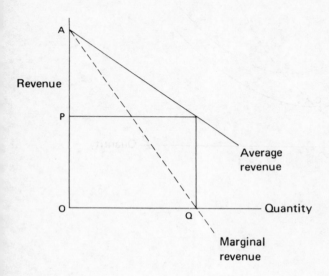

Demand is elastic

A in the price range A to P
B in the price range P to O
C in the price range A to O
D only at the price P
E nowhere in the price range shown

Questions 107 and 108 are based on the following diagram and the dimensions indicated below it. It applies to a firm in a competitive market.

ATC = average total cost
AVC = average variable cost
MC   = marginal cost

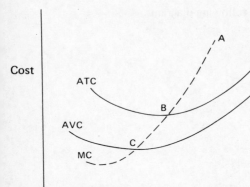

A AB
B AC
C BC
D BD
E CE

107 Which of the above is the short run supply curve?

108 Which of the above is the supply curve appropriate to the period during which fixed costs must be covered?

109 The question is based on the following diagram which shows the cost and revenue curves of an individual firm:

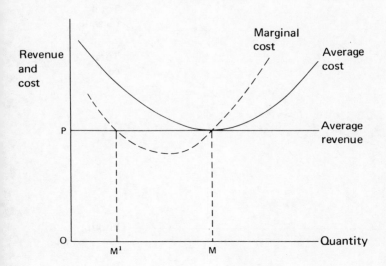

Which of the following features might be taken as an indication that the firm is operating under conditions of perfect competition?

A Marginal cost cuts average cost at the point of minimum average cost.

B Output is at the point where marginal revenue = marginal cost.

C If this were not so, output would be at OM^1 where price is equal to marginal cost.

D Average revenue = marginal revenue.

E The cost curves are U-shaped.

110 The question is based on the following diagram which shows the Total revenue and Total cost curves of an individual firm:

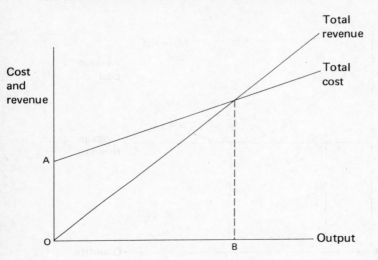

Which of the following statements are correct?

1 Marginal revenue will be less than price
2 Variable costs per unit will be constant over the range of output shown
3 OB represents the maximum profit output
4 At the output OB, price = average cost

A 1 and 2 only
B 1 and 3 only
C 2 and 3 only
D 2 and 4 only
E 3 and 4 only

111 'A decrease in price will lead to greater profits.'
Which of the following conditions are NECESSARY for this statement to be true?

1 Demand must be inelastic.
2 Total costs must be falling.
3 Demand must be elastic.
4 Marginal cost must be lower than marginal revenue.

A 1 and 2 only
B 1, 2 and 4 only
C 2 and 3 only
D 2, 3 and 4 only
E 3 and 4 only

112 All but one of the following characteristics are features of perfect competition. Which is the EXCEPTION?

A The output of any single firm is a negligibly small part of the total output of the industry.
B The product of each firm is a perfect substitute for the products of the other firms in the industry.
C There are no barriers to the entry of new firms into the industry.
D All the firms in the industry agree to charge the same price.
E Each buyer knows the prices being charged by all the firms in the industry.

Questions 113–116 are based on the following possible developments in the production and marketing conditions for Commodity X:

A The development of a close substitute for Commodity X
B Competitive advertising for Commodity X
C An increase in the price of raw materials
D Branding of Commodity X
E An effective productivity agreement with the labour force producing Commodity X

Which of the above would have any of the following effects?

113 Tend to make the demand curve more elastic

114 Tend to make the demand curve move to the right

115 Move the supply curve to the left

116 Move the supply curve to the right

117 For the monopolist, the output which yields maximum profits is always to be found

1 where $AR = MR = AC = MC$
2 where demand is elastic
3 where the extra revenue per unit is just equal to the extra cost per unit

Which of the statements are correct?

A 1, 2 and 3
B 1 and 2
C 2 and 3
D 1 only
E 3 only

118 The main task of the Monopolies Commission is to

A enforce the rules of fair competition
B break up large unified monopolies into a number of competing units
C give rulings, which have the force of law, on the operation of restrictive trade practices
D investigate, report, and make recommendations on monopolies and proposed mergers
E supervise the operations of the nationalised industries

119 Which of the following conditions are necessary in order to make price discrimination *possible*?

1 Restrictions on the buyers' ability to move from one market to the other
2 Restrictions on the movement of the goods (or services) from one market to the other
3 Different price elasticities of demand in each market

A 1, 2 and 3
B 1 and 2 only
C 2 and 3 only
D 1 only
E 3 only

Questions 120–123 are based on the following diagrams which show prices and outputs in different market situations:

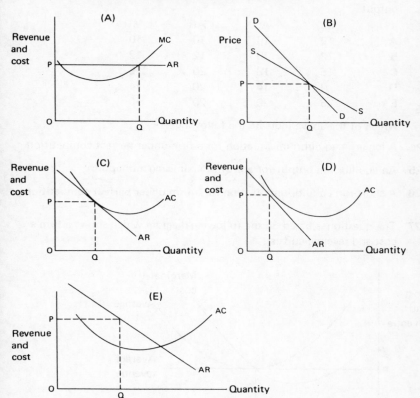

Which of the diagrams indicate the following conditions?

120 The output of the firm under perfect competition

121 A monopoly situation with abnormal profits

122 Equilibrium of the firm under conditions of imperfect competition (no restrictions on entry)

123 A nationalised industry operating under conditions of increasing returns and basing prices on marginal cost

Questions 124–126 are based on the following table. The values (in £s) of MC, AC, AR, and MR, on each line, refer to a particular level of output.

	MC	AC	AR	MR
A	10	10	10	10
B	12	9	12	12
C	15	18	20	15
D	9	14	20	14
E	25	20	20	10

Which of the above indicate the following?

124 A long-run equilibrium situation for a firm under perfect competition

125 An equilibrium output for a profit-maximising monopolist

126 A short-run equilibrium position for a firm under perfect competition

127 The question is based on the following diagram which shows a firm's cost and revenue curves:

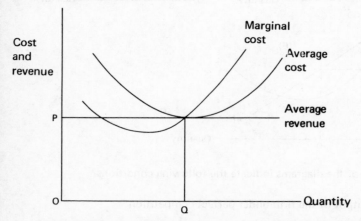

With reference to this diagram, which is the INCORRECT statement?

A OP is the long-term equilibrium price
B marginal revenue = average revenue
C at prices higher than OP the firm would make abnormal profits
D at outputs less than OQ, average revenue is greater than marginal revenue
E when the output is OQ, marginal revenue = marginal cost

Questions 128–131 refer to different types of market situation:

A The footwear industry where there are a large number of firms supplying very similar, but differentiated, goods which are sold under brand names

B A nationalised industry which is the sole buyer of certain types of electrical goods

C A trade union for skilled men which has almost 100% membership of the appropriate craftsmen

D Three very large motor-car firms which, together, supply 90% of the market in medium priced saloon cars

E An extremely efficient market in existing securities such as the London Stock Exchange

To which of the following market forms do the examples approximate?

128 Oligopoly

129 Perfect competition

130 Monopsony

131 Monopolistic competition

Questions 132–134 refer to the following equalities:

A AR = MR
B AC = MC
C AR = AC
D MR = MC

Which of these equalities

132 would apply at all outputs for the firm operating under perfect competition

133 determines the output which yields only normal profits

134 would apply for all outputs when the industry's product is being sold at a statutory fixed price.

Questions 135–137 are based on the following diagram which shows the cost and revenue curves for **an industry**:

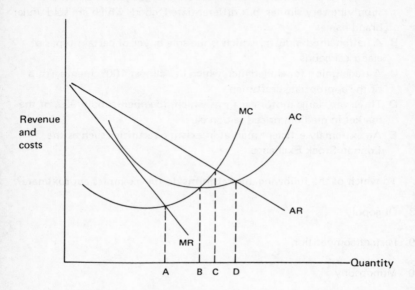

Which would be the equilibrium output if the industry were:

135 Operating under conditions of perfect competition

136 Controlled by a profit-maximising monopolist

137 A nationalised industry aiming to break even

Assertion—Reason questions

Key	First statement	Second statement
A	True	True, and correct explanation of the first statement
B	True	True, but **not** a correct explanation of first statement
C	True	False
D	False	True
E	False	False

	First statement	*Second statement*
138	Monopolies will always charge higher prices than firms in competitive industries.	A monopolist has the power to restrict the market supply and hence raise the market price.
139	Oligopoly tends to be characterised by non-price competition.	Under oligopoly any unilateral price increase leaves the individual firm worse off, any price reduction which is multilateral leaves all firms worse off.
140	In the long-run equilibrium situation under conditions of imperfect competition, the firm will be earning only normal profits.	Under imperfect competition the individual firm in the long-run equilibrium will be producing less than its optimum output.
141	Under perfect competition, firms will aim to produce where AC = MC.	When AR = MR, a profit-maximising firm will always produce where AC is at a minimum.

6 National income

Questions 142 and 143 are based on this simple diagram which is intended to show the values of the output at the four different stages of the production of a commodity. Stage 4 is the retail stage and Stage 1 is the first process in the sequence of production activities.

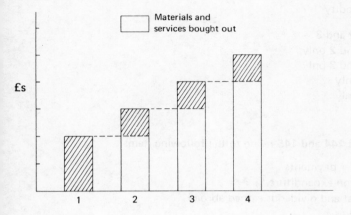

£s

Materials and
services bought out

1   2   3   4

142 For purposes of computing the contribution to national income we could

1 sum the total values of the output of each stage
2 sum the values represented by the unshaded areas
3 sum the values represented by the shaded areas
4 take the value of the final stage only
5 use the sum of the shaded areas minus the sum of the unshaded areas

A 1 or 2
B 2 or 3
C 3 or 4
D 3 or 5
E 4 or 5

143 Which of the following statements is correct?

The sum of the shaded areas is equal to

1 the value of the final product
2 the sum of the values added at each stage
3 the value of the incomes generated in the production of the commodity

    A 1, 2 and 3
    B 1 and 2 only
    C 2 and 3 only
    D 1 only
    E 3 only

Questions 144 and 145 relate to the following items:

1 Transfer payments
2 Taxes on expenditure
3 Interest and dividends earned abroad
4 Subsidies
5 Profits retained by companies
6 Exports
7 Imports
8 Employers' National Insurance contributions
9 The value of physical increase in stocks and work in progress

144 Which of these items must be counted as part of the national income when it is measured by the income method?

    A 1, 3, 5 and 6 only
    B 3, 4, 5 and 6 only
    C 3, 5 and 6 only
    D 3, 5 and 8 only
    E 4, 5, 6 and 8 only

145 In computing the gross national product at factor cost from the basis of national expenditure, some of these items would enter and some would be subtracted. Which would be subtracted?

A 1 and 2 only
B 1, 7 and 9 only
C 2, 4, 7 and 9 only
D 2 and 7 only
E 4 and 7 only

Questions 146–150 are based on the following diagram:

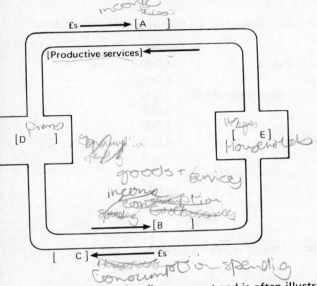

National income is a flow concept and is often illustrated by a flow diagram similar to the one above.

Indicate the correct location, on this diagram, of the following terms:

146 Firms

147 Wages, interest, rent and profit

148 Consumption spending

149 Households

150 Goods and services

151 National income is equal to

A gross national product at factor cost
B gross national product at market prices — capital consumption
C gross domestic product at factor cost + net income from abroad
D gross national product at market prices — taxes on expenditure
E gross domestic product at factor cost + net income from abroad — capital consumption

Questions 152—154 are based on the following hypothetical data:

	£million
Consumers' expenditure	20,000
Gross investment	6,000
Public authorities' current spending	6,000
Exports	5,000
Imports	7,000
Taxes on expenditure	4,000
Subsidies	500
Net property income from abroad	500
Depreciation	2,000

152 The gross national product at market prices is

A 30,000
B 30,500
C 35,500
D 37,500
E 39,500

153 The gross national product at factor cost is

A 25,000
B 27,000
C 29,000
D 30,500
E 37,500

154 The national income at factor cost is

    A 25,000
    B 25,500
    C 27,000
    D 29,000
    E 33,500

155 Which of the following items would be counted as part of the national income?

    1 A prize in the premium bonds lottery
    2 A housekeeper's salary
    3 The pay of a policeman
    4 Unemployment pay
    5 Profits retained by companies
    6 The income of a used-car salesman

        A 1, 3, 4 and 6 only
        B 2 and 3 only
        C 2, 3, 4 and 5 only
        D 2, 3, 5 and 6 only
        E 3 and 5 only

156 The following details have been extracted from the national income accounts of an imaginary country. What is the national income? Note that all the items shown will not be required for your calculation.

Income from employment	100
Income from self-employment	20
Rent, interest, dividends	20
Undistributed profits and surpluses	10
Taxes on income	20
Social security benefits	20
Exports	20
Imports	30
Net property income from abroad	10
Depreciation	10

    A 170   C 140   E 120
    B 150   D 130

7 Incomes

Wages
Rent
Profits
Interest

157 In which of the following industrial situations is the demand for labour likely to be fairly elastic?

1 An industry where labour costs form a small proportion of total costs
2 An industry in which technical progress is continually developing inexpensive labour-saving techniques
3 An industry producing a commodity which has a very inelastic demand
4 An industry which is labour-intensive and supplies a commodity which has a very elastic demand

A 1 and 2 only
B 1 and 3 only
C 2 and 3 only
D 2 and 4 only
E 3 and 4 only

158 'Architects are highly paid because they have to undergo a long period of training.'

As an explanation of wage determination, this statement is

A true, because a person who undertakes a long period of training deserves a high reward
B true, because greater skill merits higher pay
C false, because it ignores the conditions of supply
D inadequate, because it considers only one of the conditions of supply
E inadequate, because the length of training has no bearing on the short-term supply conditions

159 'Wage drift' refers to

A the movement of wages when there is no effective incomes policy
B the difference in the levels of wages as between different industries
C the difference between the movements in wages and the movements in earnings, excluding the effect of overtime
D regional variations in wage rates
E the situation where one group of workers obtains a wage increase because wages have risen in a comparable occupation

160 The diagram shows the MRP of labour to the individual profit-maximising firm. Labour is the only variable factor and there is perfect competition in the labour market.

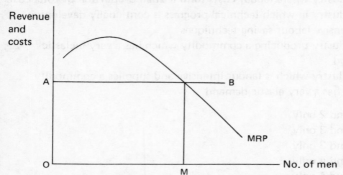

The firm maximises its profits by employing OM workers. The line AB, therefore, represents

1 the MC of labour
2 the AC of labour
3 the ruling wage rate

    A 1, 2 and 3
    B 1 and 2 only
    C 2 and 3 only
    D 1 only
    E 3 only

161 The diagram shows the supply curve for a particular type of labour. Demand has increased from DD to D'D'.

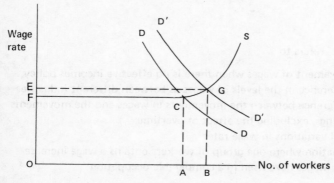

Which of the following areas represents the element of economic rent in the total remuneration?

A Area GEOB

B Area GEFC

C Area CFOA

D Area GCAB

162 The question is based on the following data:

	Year 1	Year 5
Wage rate (per hour)	300p	360p
Price index	130	120

During the interval of time given, real wages have

A risen by 10%

B risen by 20%

C risen by 30%

D remained constant

E fallen by 10%

163 Transfer earnings are

A the level of earnings which is required to tempt factors of production away from their present employment

B that part of the earnings of a factor of production which is classed as economic rent

C the minimum payment necessary to retain factors of production in their present employment

D payments in the form of pensions and social security benefits

E payments made to labour during periods of retraining

164 A plot of land in the centre of a city could earn a rental of £1,000 per annum in its least remunerative occupation. It earns, in fact, £3,500 per annum in its present use.

Which of the following statements is correct?

A The economic rent is £2,500.
B There is no economic rent because land is geographically immobile.
C The economic rent is £3,500.
D There is no economic rent because there are no transfer earnings.
E The economic rent cannot be determined from the facts given.

165 Which of the following is NOT characteristic of a situation where economic rent is present?

A Price increases as demand increases.
B If demand increases, price will exceed transfer earnings.
C If demand falls, price remains unchanged.
D In the short run supply is inelastic.
E A tax which does not exceed the rent element will not affect the price.

166 The question is based on the following financial data:

	Sales	Profit as a % of turnover	Capital employed
Company A	£100,000	10%	£50,000
Company B	£1,000,000	20%	£2,000,000
Company C	£600,000	5%	£1,000,000

Which of the following sequences ranks these companies in order of the returns they earn on the capital employed — that company earning the greatest return being placed first?

A B, A, C
B C, A, B
C A, B, C
D C, B, A
E A, C, B

167 All but one of the following features may be said to be characteristics of profits. Which is the EXCEPTION?

    A A contractual payment fixed in advance.of the service rendered
    B Uncertain in amount
    C A residual item
    D A reward for innovation
    E May be negative

168 The phrase 'the supply price of entrepreneurship' refers to

    A rent of ability
    B normal profits
    C abnormal profits
    D rent of monopoly
    E salaries of management personnel

Questions 169–172 refer to the various functions and features of profits:

    A An incentive to undertake risky enterprises
    B A guide to potential investors
    C A windfall gain due to inflation
    D A source of investment funds
    E A return resulting from contrived scarcity

To which of the above categories would you assign the following illustrations?

169 'There is a fortune awaiting the firm which produces the first effective low-cost electric car.'

170 'A monopolist can use his control of the market to earn abnormal profits.'

171 'Most of the new development in the motor-car industry has been financed by the method of ploughing back.'

172 'The disappointing sales of coal-fired appliances have caused several firms to leave the industry.'

173 Which of the following equalities apply at the long-run equilibrium output under conditions of imperfect (monopolistic) competition?

1 AR = MR
2 AR = AC
3 MR = MC
4 AC = MC

A 1 and 2
B 1 and 3
C 2 and 3
D 2 and 4
E 3 and 4

174 The question refers to the following possible changes within an industry:

1 An increase in wage rates
2 A shortening of the working week with no reduction in wages
3 A longer annual paid holiday

In the event of all these changes taking place, we have sufficient information here to say that

A labour costs per unit of output will rise
B profits will fall
C the price of the product will increase
D there will be some fall in employment
E no conclusions can be drawn regarding the movements in costs, prices and profits

175 Other things being equal, an increase in liquidity preference will lead to

A a fall in the supply of money
B an increase in the supply of loanable funds
C a fall in the rate of interest
D increased holdings of money
E none of the above

176. In order to start his own business a man withdraws his savings of £20,000 from a deposit account in which it is earning a rate of interest of 10%. His potential earnings as an employee are £6,000 per annum. In his first year his accounts show total expenses of £12,000 and total sales revenue of £30,000. His true profit for the year is

A £18,000
B £16,000
C £14,000
D £12,000
E £10,000

177 When the market price of 2½% Consols stands at 40, the yield on the stock would be

A 5%
B 5¼%
C 5½%
D 6¼%
E 10%

178 A fall in the market price of fixed interest securities is an indication that

A the market rate of interest has risen
B the market rate of interest has fallen
C liquidity preference has decreased
D the supply of money has increased
E the banks are operating a more liberal lending policy

179 Which of the following assertions regarding the effects of an increase in the rate of interest are correct?

1 It will increase the future income obtainable for a given sacrifice of current satisfactions.
2 It will reduce the present value of future income.
3 It will mean that a given future income can be obtained for a smaller reduction in current spending.

    A 1, 2 and 3
    B 1 and 2 only
    C 2 and 3 only
    D 1 only
    E 3 only

180 When the market rate of interest is 5%, the present discounted value of £100 payable one year from now is

    A £95
    B £95.24
    C £95.56
    D £96.24
    E £105

181 The marginal efficiency of capital is normally expressed in

    A units of output
    B units of output per unit of time
    C units of money
    D units of money per unit of time
    E terms of a percentage return

Key	First statement	Second statement
A	True	True, and correct explanation of first statement
B	True	True, but *not* a correct explanation of second statement
C	True	False
D	False	True
E	False	False

182 During inflation an increase in the rate of interest may have little effect on the demand for loanable funds.

If prices are rising sharply the real rate of interest will be much lower than the nominal rate.

183 If the supply of a factor of production is perfectly inelastic, a tax levied on its earnings will not affect the market price of the factor.

When supply is perfectly inelastic a change in demand will alter the quantity supplied but not the price.

184 Normal profits may be regarded as a form of economic rent.

Normal profits represent the entrepreneur's transfer earnings.

185 If labour were perfectly mobile both occupationally and geographically, money wage differentials as between different occupations would disappear.

In the real world, if the non-monetary rewards and penalties as well as the money wages of different occupations were taken into account, we should find that the net advantages of different occupations were equal.

8 Money and banking

Structure of bank assets
Central bank controls

Questions 186—189 refer to the following assets of the commercial banks:

Cash   A
Money at call   B
Bills discounted   C
Investments   D
Advances   E

Only one letter is required for each answer.

186 Which of the above items is the most illiquid asset?

187 Which of the items is the most profitable asset?

188 Which item is equal to about one half of the value of total deposits?

189 Which item contains the commercial banks' deposits at the Bank of England?

Questions 190—193 refer to the following assets of the commercial banks:

1 Cash in the banks' tills
2 Operational deposits held at the Bank of England
3 Loans to the discount houses
4 Overdrafts incurred by large industrial companies
5 Holdings of government securities with maturities between five and ten years
6 Holdings of commercial bills of exchange
7 Holdings of Treasury Bills
8 Special deposits at the Bank of England

190 Which of these items should be regarded as cash?

A 1 only
B 1 and 2 only
C 1, 2 and 3 only
D 1, 2 and 7 only
E 1, 2 and 8 only

191 Which of the items comprise the banks' liquid assets?

A 1, 2 and 3 only
B 1, 3 and 6 only
C 1, 2, 3, 6 and 7 only
D 1, 2, 3, 5, 6 and 7 only
E 1, 2, 3, 4, 7 and 8 only

192 Which of the items comes into being as the result of the Bank of England using its most direct monetary control?

A 2
B 3
C 5
D 7
E 8

193 Which item would appear under the heading 'Money at call and short notice'?

A 2
B 3
C 6
D 7
E 8

194 Which of the following will NOT appear on the liabilities side of a bank's balance sheet?

A Deposits held on current account (i.e. sight deposits)
B Time deposits
C The share capital of the bank
D Loans to customers

195 The banks, in a multi-bank system, maintain a minimum cash ratio of 10%. An individual bank receives a cash deposit of £1,000. On the basis of this additional cash this particular bank will feel able to create **additional** deposits equal to

A   £10,000
B   £9,000
C   £1,100
D   £1,000
E   £900

196 The banking regulations introduced by the Bank of England in 1981

1 abolished the reserve assets ratio
2 obliged all banks to maintain operational balances at the Bank of England equal to 1½% of their eligible liabilities
3 abolished the special deposits scheme

Which of the above statements is/are correct?

A 1, 2 and 3
B 1 and 2 only
C 2 and 3 only
D 1 only
E 3 only

197 When a bank makes a loan to an existing account holder

1 its assets increase by the amount of the loan
2 its liabilities increase by the amount of the loan
3 other things remaining equal, the money supply increases

A 1, 2 and 3
B 1 and 2 only
C 2 and 3 only
D 1 only
E 3 only

198 The question is based on the following monetary features:

1 An increase in the special deposits held by the Bank of England
2 The Bank of England sells securities in the open market
3 The Bank of England buys securities in the open market
4 A large-scale funding operation
5 A significant decrease in the hoarding of cash

Which of these events would reduce the commercial banks' ability to lend?

A 2 and 4 only
B 3 and 5 only
C 1, 2 and 4 only
D 1, 3 and 4 only
E 1, 2, 4 and 5 only

199 Which of the following would appear on the liabilities side of the balance sheet of a commercial bank?

1 Time deposits of customers
2 Retained profits
3 Certificates of deposit issued by the bank

A 1, 2 and 3
B 1 and 2 only
C 2 and 3 only
D 1 only
E 3 only

Questions 200—203 are based on the following items which appear on the weekly return from the Banking Department of the Bank of England (NB. Certain items have been omitted from this return):

Liabilities
1 Public deposits
2 Special deposits
3 Bankers' deposits

Assets
4 Government securities
5 Notes and coin

A 1 increases   3 decreases
B 1 increases   5 decreases
C 2 increases   3 decreases
D 3 decreases   4 decreases
E 3 decreases   5 decreases

Which of the above combinations represent the movements which will occur as a result of the following transactions?

200 The Bank of England sells securities in the open market.

201 The Bank of England makes a call for special deposits.

202 The Inland Revenue is receiving large tax payments.

203 The clearing banks withdraw supplies of bank notes from the central bank.

204 The question is based on the following news item:

'With heavy tax transfers dominating the market yesterday, calling was heavy and widespread. The Bank gave the market a large amount of assistance.'

The item refers to the situation in

A the capital market
B the commodities markets
C the money market
D the foreign exchange market
E the Stock Exchange

Questions 205—208 are based on the following alternative hypothetical circumstances:

A Under present conditions wealth is more securely held in the form of physical assets than in money.
B Those holding wealth in the form of money have greatly benefited during the past few years.
C Increased buying of securities has caused their prices to rise.
D A reduction in the money supply has caused a decrease in security prices.
E The level of spending has risen much faster than the level of bank deposits.

Which of these statements describe:

205 A deflationary situation

206 An increase in the transactions velocity of circulation of money

207 A fall in interest rates

208 An inflationary situation

9 Public finance

The budget
Economic effects of taxation

Questions 209—211 relate to the following diagram which shows the effects of imposing a specific tax on a commodity:

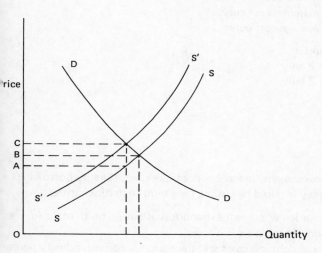

A OA
B OC
C BC
D BA
E CA

Which of the above dimensions indicates the following?

209 The amount of tax per unit of output

210 The net revenue per unit received by producers after the imposition of the tax

211 The amount of tax per unit 'passed on' to consumers.

212 When a lump sum tax is levied on the profits of a profit-maximising monopolist, it will

1 cause him to reduce his output
2 raise his marginal cost curve
3 raise his average cost curve

    A 1, 2 and 3
    B 1 and 2 only
    C 2 and 3 only
    D 1 only
    E 3 only

213 When the government finances part of its expenditure by borrowing and the money is raised by issuing long-term (dated) securities

    A the real burden of current expenditure is passed on to some future generation of taxpayers
    B the national debt increases and the nation is correspondingly poorer
    C although the debt must be repaid in the future, the real costs are incurred when the expenditure is undertaken
    D the annual interest payments reduce the national income

Questions 214–216 relate to the following taxes as currently applied under the British system of taxation:

    A Income tax
    B Corporation tax
    C Excise duty on tobacco
    D Motor vehicle duties
    E Excise duty on oil and petrol

214 Which of these taxes raises the most revenue?

215 Which tax is proportional?

216 Which tax raises the least revenue?

Questions 217—221 are based on the following details taken from the budget estimates for the year 1982—83:

Revenue	£m	Expenditure	£m
Inland Revenue		D	13,945
A	30,775	Health	10,260
B	4,850	E	11,768
Petroleum revenue tax	4,330	Rate Support Grant	16,087
Capital gains tax	600	Housing	2,318
Customs and Excise			
C	14,750		
Oil	5,100		
Tobacco	3,525		

Which of the items A to E represent

217 Value added tax?

218 Defence?

219 Social security?

220 Income tax?

221 Corporation tax?

222 An overall budget deficit will

1 tend to increase aggregate demand
2 probably increase the national debt
3 reduce the fiduciary issue

A 1, 2 and 3
B 1 and 2 only
C 2 and 3 only
D 3 only
E 1 only

Questions 223–225 are based on the following diagram:

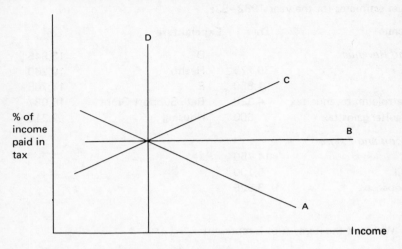

Which of the lines represents the following?

223 A progressive tax

224 A proportional tax

225 A regressive tax

Questions 226 and 227 are based on the following items of public expenditure in the UK:

A Defence
B Social services
C Aids to industry and agriculture
D The Civil Service
E Overseas aid

226 Which is the largest of the above items of public expenditure?

227 Which of the above, in recent years, has been the fastest growing item of public expenditure?

Questions 228–230 are based on the following hypothetical changes in taxation:

A   A reduction in income tax
B   An increase in corporation tax
C   A decrease in indirect taxation
D   An increase in capital gains tax
E   An increase in capital transfer tax

28   Which of the changes would lead to a fall in the Index of Retail Prices?

29   Which change would tend to increase the inequality in the distribution of disposable incomes?

30   Which of the changes might be described as 'making the distribution of the tax burden more regressive'?

31 | Gross Annual Income (£) | Tax Paid to Inland Revenue (£) |
|---|---|
| 4,000 | 400 |
| 5,000 | 450 |
| 6,000 | 480 |
| 7,000 | 490 |

The tax illustrated above is

A   indirect and progressive
B   direct and progressive
C   indirect and regressive
D   direct and proportional
E   direct and regressive

232 The question refers to the following quotation:

'An increase in indirect taxation which leads to an increase in prices can hardly be described as a deflationary measure.'

If we assume no cost-push effects, however, the policy will be deflationary if

A the taxes are imposed on goods with an inelastic demand
B the taxes are placed on goods which have untaxed close substitutes
C the taxes are placed on goods which have elastic demands
D incomes are rising faster than prices (including the taxes)
E the increased taxes are offset by increased government current spending

10 The determination of income

Aggregate demand
Leakages and injections
The multiplier
Equilibrium levels of income

233 The marginal propensity to consume is

    A the actual amount of any increment of income which is spent on consumption

    B the proportion of total income spent on consumption goods and services

    C the proportion of any increment of income which is spent on consumption

    D the reciprocal of the marginal propensity to save

    E the actual level of consumption spending

234 In a two-sector economy the relationship between the marginal propensity to save and the marginal propensity to consume is that

    A their sum is equal to aggregate demand

    B their sum is equal to the value of the multiplier

    C their sum is equal to unity

    D they both move in the same direction

    E there is no relationship between them

235 When the marginal propensity to consume is ¾, and the marginal propensity to import is $1/12$, then, assuming no government activity, the value of the multiplier is

    A 4

    B $1\frac{1}{5}$

    C 3

    D 1¼

    E 6

236 In an economy with no inflationary pressures, other things being equal, an increase in the propensity to save will

    A increase the planned rate of investment

    B increase the level of saving

    C increase the level of income

    D leave the volume of saving unchanged

    E make the multiplier larger

Questions 237–239 are based on the following diagram, in which CC represents the propensity to consume:

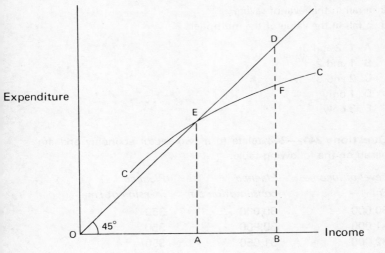

A OA
B DE
C EA
D DF
E AB

Which of the above dimensions represents:

237 Savings

238 The level of consumption when saving is zero

239 Assume investment is now introduced into the above situation, what level of investment is required to raise income from OA to OB?

240 Assuming no change in the propensity to consume, the effect of a fall in investment will be

1 a fall in the level of income
2 a fall in the level of saving
3 a fall in the value of the multiplier

  A 1, 2 and 3
  B 1 and 2
  C 2 and 3
  D 1 only
  E 3 only

Questions 241—243 relate to a two-sector economy and are based on the following table:

Level of income £m	Planned consumption £m	Planned investment £m
30,000	30,000	350
31,000	30,900	350
32,000	31,650	350
33,000	32,150	350
34,000	32,450	350

241 What is the value of the marginal propensity to save as income rises from £31,000m to £32,000m?

  A 0.5
  B 0.25
  C 0.75
  D 0.3
  E 0.15

242 What is the value of the marginal propensity to consume as income rises from £32,000m to £33,000m?

  A 0.25
  B 0.3
  C 0.5
  D 0.75
  E 1.0

243 Which level of income represents an equilibrium situation?

    A £30,000m

    B £31,000m

    C £32,000m

    D £33,000m

    E £34,000m

244 In a two-sector economy equilibrium income is that level at which

    A realised saving is equal to realised investment

    B full employment exists

    C planned consumption plus planned savings is equal to planned investment

    D the amount which the community desires to invest is equal to the amount which it does not wish to spend

    E income is equal to planned leakages plus planned injections

Questions 245–248 are based on the following diagram in which II represents investment spending and SS shows the movements in savings;

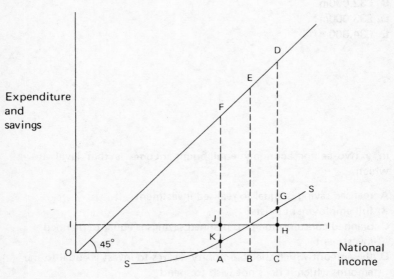

A GH
B OB
C JK
D DG
E FJ

Which of the above dimensions represents:

245 Excess demand?

246 Excess supply?

247 The equilibrium level of income?

248 Consumption spending?

249 The question is based on the following diagram:

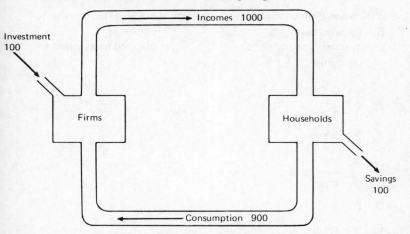

The diagram shows an equilibrium situation. If we now assume that the planned rate of investment rises by 50, and that APS = MPS what will be the new equilibrium level of income?

A   500
B   1,000
C   1,050
D   1,500
E   2,000

250 An increase in aggregate demand is not likely to lead to an increase in employment when

1   the increased demand is for exports
2   there is excess capacity in the economy
3   aggregate supply is completely inelastic
4   the increased demand is for imports
5   the extra demand takes the form of increased government spending

Which statements are correct?

A   1 and 5 only
B   3 and 4 only
C   1, 2 and 3 only
D   1, 2 and 5 only
E   3, 4 and 5 only

Questions 251—254 are based on the following expressions in which

Y = national income
S = planned savings
c = average propensity to
  consume

mpc = marginal propensity to
  consume
I = planned investment

A $\dfrac{1}{1-mpc}$

B $Y - cY = I$

C $\dfrac{1}{1-mpc} \times I$

D $S > I$

E $Y = c + S$

For a two-sector economy (no government activity, no foreign trade),
which of the above expressions represents:

251 The multiplier

252 A situation which will lead to a fall in national income

253 The condition for an equilibrium level of income

254 The actual size of the national income

Questions 255—257 are based on the following data:

Exports (X) = 200
Imports (M) = 150
Investment (I) = 100
Consumption (C) = 700

Government spending on goods and
  services (G) = 150
Taxation (T) = 100
Savings (S) = 200
National income (Y) = 1,000

255 On the basis of this data we can deduce that

  A national income is at an equilibrium level
  B national income is not in equilibrium; it will be expanding
  C national income is not in equilibrium; it will be contracting
  D there is insufficient evidence to draw any conclusions about
     equilibrium

256 What is the level of leakages from the circular flow of income?

  A 200
  B 300
  C 350
  D 450
  E 800

257 What is the level of aggregate demand?

  A   700
  B   800
  C   900
  D 1,000
  E 1,150

Questions 258–261 are based on the following hypothetical circumstances:

A A large localised industry suffers the loss of some of its major export markets

B Aggregate demand for consumer goods is maintained at a relatively high level but changes in income and taste are causing significant movements in the composition of the total demand

C A nation which has a large export business begins to feel the effects of a major depression in world trade

D Winter conditions greatly reduce the output of the building industry

E A motor-car firm switches a large part of its production from the home market to the export market

Which of these circumstances might provide an example of:

258 Cyclical unemployment

259 Seasonal unemployment

260 Structural unemployment

261 Frictional unemployment

262 The paradox of thrift refers to the fact that

A saving may decrease as income increases

B an increased propensity to save may lead to a fall in realised saving

C an increase in saving may cause national income to rise

D an increase in saving causes an increase in investment

Assertion—Reason questions

Key	First statement	Second statement
A	True	True, and correct explanation of the first statement
B	True	True, but **not** a correct explanation of the second statement
C	True	False

Key	First statement	Second statement
D	False	True
E	False	False

263 The multiplier only applies when changes take place in investment spending.

A rise in investment spending brings about greater changes in income because it stimulates secondary changes in consumer spending.

264 The size of the multiplier depends on the marginal rate of leakage from the circular flow of income.

Only that part of new income which is respent on domestic output can generate additions to national income.

265 Changes in saving and changes in exports will have similar effects on the level of income.

Output which leaves the country reduces domestic incomes in the same way as the act of saving.

266 If government expenditure is greater than the yield from taxation, income cannot be in equilibrium.

Equilibrium requires that total leakages should equal total injections.

267 A proportional income tax acts as a built-in stabiliser.

A proportional income tax withdraws more income from the circular flow when income rises and less when income falls.

11 International trade

The law of comparative costs
The terms of trade
The balance of payments
Devaluation
International economic cooperation

268 The question is based on the following production possibilities:

	Tons of wheat		No. of tractors
With 1 unit of resources country A can produce	10	or	6
With 1 unit of resources country B can produce	8	or	4

This situation provides

A no basis for the trade because A is more efficient at producing both commodities

B no basis for trade because the situation is one of absolute advantage and not comparative advantage

C a basis for trade on terms which lie between 10 wheat for 4 tractors and 8 wheat for 6 tractors

D a basis for trade on terms which lie between 5 wheat for 3 tractors and 2 wheat for 1 tractor

E no basis for trade because the domestic opportunity cost ratios are different

269 In country A, commodity X costs £1 per unit and commodity Y costs £2 per unit. In country B commodity X costs $2.5 per unit and commodity Y costs $5 per unit. If trading opportunities arose

A country A would export X and import Y

B country B would export X and import Y

C both countries would try to export X

D both countries would try to export Y

E no trade in X and Y would occur

Questions 270–272 refer to the following data concerning the production possibilities in two countries:

	Units of resources required	
	Country A	Country B
To produce 1 tractor	30	60
To produce 1 ton of wheat	10	40

270 With respect to trade possibilities

A country B has an absolute advantage in the production of tractors
B country A has a comparative advantage in the production of tractors
C country B has an absolute advantage in the production of wheat
D country B has a comparative advantage in the production of wheat
E none of the above statements is correct

271 Assume that the currency in country A is pounds and in country B it is dollars. Before trade, the price of tractors in A is £450, and the price of 1 ton of wheat in B is $600. In equilibrium, therefore, assuming perfect competition the other prices will be

	Price of 1 ton of wheat in A (£)	Price of tractors in B ($)
A	1,350	1,200
B	150	900
C	300	400
D	900	800
E	500	600

272 If 1 unit of resources costs £15 in country A and $15 in country B, then balanced trade is possible and advantageous to both countries if the exchange rate is

A £1 = $3
B £1 = $2
C £1 = $1
D £1 = $4
E none of the above since country A is more efficient in both industries

273 The question is based on the following diagram in which X represents the country's equilibrium position before trade and Y the equilibrium after trade:

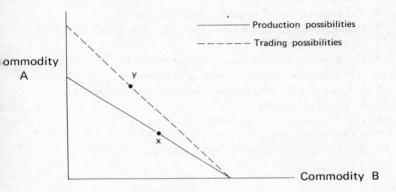

In moving from X to Y the country will

1 export commodity A and import commodity B
2 export commodity B and import commodity A
3 now consume more of both commodities
4 specialise in the production of commodity A
5 specialise in the production of commodity B

Which of these statements are correct?

A 1 and 4 only
B 2 and 4 only
C 2 and 5 only
D 1, 3 and 4 only
E 2, 3 and 5 only

274 A favourable movement in the terms of trade means

A the balance of trade has moved favourably
B the volume of exports has risen relative to the volume of imports
C the revenue from exports has risen relative to the expenditure on imports
D the prices of exports have risen relative to the prices of imports
E the value of the home currency has depreciated in the foreign exchange markets

Questions 275—277 are based on the following items and their roles in the British balance of payments:

1 The sale of British motor-cars to foreign buyers
2 The expenditure of American tourists in Britain
3 Immigrants in Britain sending monetary gifts to relatives in their former homeland
4 The payment of royalties, by foreigners, on British patents
5 A twenty-year loan to a foreign government
6 The sale of a British company overseas to a foreign firm
7 A loan from the IMF
8 The purchase of foreign foodstuffs
9 An increase in the foreign currency reserves
10 Buying local services for British troops stationed abroad

275 Which items will appear in the Balance of Trade?

A 1 only
B 1 and 8 only
C 1, 2, 4 and 8 only
D 1, 4, 6 and 8 only
E 1, 4, 8 and 10 only

276 Which items will appear in the Invisible Account?

A 2, 3 and 4 only
B 2, 4 and 10 only
C 2, 3, 4 and 10 only
D 2, 4, 6 and 7 only
E 3, 6, 7 and 10 only

277 Which items are placed in the Official Financing section?

A 9 only
B 7 and 9 only
C 2, 3 and 4 only
D 2, 4, 7 and 10 only
E 6, 7, 9 and 10 only

Questions 278—280 are based on the following hypothetical balance of payments situation:

1	Imports	− 5,000
2	Exports	+ 4,500
3	Interest, profits and dividends	+ 500
4	Long-term investment overseas (net)	− 200
5	Government current spending overseas (net)	− 500
6	Balancing item	60
7	Other invisibles	+ 400
8	Change in reserves	40
9	Other monetary movements	200

278 The balance of payments on current account is

A a surplus of 100
B a deficit of 100
C a surplus of 200
D a deficit of 500
E a surplus of 400

279 Which are the 'invisible items'?

A 2 and 7 only
B 3, 5 and 7 only
C 2, 4, 6 and 7
D 2, 5, 7 and 8
E 3, 5, 7 and 9

280 The correct signs for items 6, 8 and 9 are

A − 60 + 40 + 200
B + 60 − 40 − 200
C − 60 − 40 − 200
D + 60 + 40 + 200
E + 60 − 40 + 200

281 Country X devalues. The elasticity of demand for her exports is 2. Her demand for imports has an elasticity of ½.

Neglecting income effects and assuming the elasticities of supply are infinite, which of the following statements are correct?

1 Export earnings (in foreign currency) will fall.
2 Expenditure (in foreign currency) on imports will fall.
3 Export earnings (in foreign currency) will rise.
4 Expenditure (in foreign currency) on imports will rise.

    A 1 and 2 only
    B 1 and 4 only
    C 2 and 3 only
    D 3 and 4 only
    E No combination of these statements

282 Which combination of the following changes represents an improvement in the terms of trade?

1 Export prices rise by 8%
2 Export prices fall by 5%
3 Import prices rise by 10%
4 Import prices rise by 5%

    A 1 and 3
    B 1 and 4
    C 2 and 3
    D 2 and 4

Questions 283 and 284 relate to the following situation:
A country which plays a significant part in world trade is experiencing rather severe inflation and its domestic price level is rising faster than world prices.

283 Assuming this country to be operating a fixed exchange rate, which of the following are likely consequences?

1 A fall in the foreign exchange reserves
2 A rise in the foreign exchange reserves

3 The central bank intervenes in the foreign exchange market to buy the home currency

4 The central bank intervenes in the foreign exchange market to sell the home currency

    A 1 and 3
    B 1 and 4
    C 2 and 3
    D 2 and 4

284 If this same country were on a floating rate of exchange, which of the following price effects would occur?

	In terms of home currency	*In terms of foreign currency*
A	Exports cheaper	Imports dearer
B	Imports cheaper	Exports cheaper
C	Exports dearer	Imports dearer
D	Imports dearer	Exports cheaper

285 The question is based on the following quotation:

'Devaluation has given British industry a great opportunity to export more. In order to ensure that industry seizes this opportunity, the government must encourage a movement of resources to the exporting sectors.'

Which of the following statements are relevant to this quotation?

1 British goods have become cheaper in terms of foreign currencies.

2 Foreign goods have become dearer in terms of foreign currencies.

3 Devaluation provides an added measure of protection to home producers.

4 A restriction of home demand increases the supply of exports.

5 There will be a significant increase in foreign currency earnings if the demand for British goods in foreign markets is inelastic.

    A 1 and 4 only
    B 1, 2 and 4 only
    C 1, 3 and 4 only
    D 1, 3, 4 and 5 only
    E 1, 2, 3, 4 and 5

286 Britain repays a loan to IMF. Other things remaining equal, which of the following statements describe the effects of the transaction?

1 Britain's sterling liabilities are increased
2 Britain's gold and foreign currency reserves are reduced
3 The IMF's reserves of sterling are reduced

A 1, 2, 3
B 1 and 2 only
C 2 and 3 only
D 1 only
E 3 only

287 Which of the following are included in the UK's official reserves?

1 Unconditional drawing rights on the IMF
2 Treasury Bills
3 Convertible foreign currencies
4 Special deposits
5 SDRs

A 1, 2 and 4
B 1, 3 and 4
C 1, 3 and 5
D 2, 3 and 5
E 2, 4 and 5

288 Which of the following conditions is most desirable if international trade is to be conducted on a multilateral basis?

A Abolition of tariffs
B Fixed exchange rates
C International harmonisation of taxation policies
D Full convertibility of currencies
E Prohibition of dumping

Questions 289—291 are concerned with the following institutions:

A GATT   B IMF   C OECD   D EFTA   E IBRD

Which of the above is concerned mainly with:

89   Reducing the major barriers to world trade

90   Rendering aid to developing countries on a long-term basis

91   Stability of exchange rates and the convertibility of currencies

92   The question is based on the following characteristics:

1   The existence of supranational institutions
2   Free trade between members
3   A common external tariff
4   Common frontiers
5   Free movement of the factors of production

Which of the features distinguish a common market from a free
trade area?

A 3 and 4 only   B 1, 3 and 5 only   C 3, 4 and 5 only
D 1, 3, 4 and 5 only   E None of the above since they are all common
features

Questions 293—295 concern a hypothetical country A, whose domestic
currency is the groat, and its relationship with the IMF.

A The IMF's holdings of currencies other than groats increases.
B Country A's normal drawing rights at the IMF have expired.
C Country A's drawing rights are restored although she has not repaid
   her loans.
D Country A is restricted to conditional drawing rights.
E The IMF declares the groat to be a scarce currency.

Which of these items might be a consequence of the following
developments?

293   Country A repays a loan from the IMF

294   The IMF's holdings of groats is equal to twice the value of country A's
      quota.

295   Country A has borrowed foreign currency equal to the value of its
      gold tranche.

12 Economic policies

Questions 296 and 297 refer to the following policies:

1 The use of licences and permits in order to obtain supplies of raw materials
2 The use of subsidies to encourage the production of milk
3 The use of taxes to raise the prices of luxury goods
4 Limiting imports by means of quotas
5 Limiting imports by means of tariffs

296 Which of these measures may be described as 'planning by direction'?

A 1 and 2 only   B 1 and 4 only   C 2 and 3 only
D 1, 2 and 3 only   E 2, 3 and 5 only

297 Which of these measures may be described as 'planning through the market'?

A 1 and 2 only   B 1 and 4 only   C 2 and 3 only
D 1, 2 and 3 only   E 2, 3 and 5 only

298 The term 'fiscal policy' means

A the use of the central banks' powers to vary the amount of bank lending in order to control the amount of spending
B the control of incomes and prices so as to prevent inflation
C government measures to change the levels of imports and exports
D the adjustment of taxation and public expenditure so as to influence aggregate demand

299 Which of the following may be said to be long-term aims of incomes policies such as those operated in Britain in recent years?

1 To stimulate a steady growth in real national output
2 To freeze existing differentials
3 To bring about equality of incomes
4 To allow incomes to rise at the same rate as prices
5 To protect the less well-organised groups in the community
6 To correct a lack of balance between movements in money income and real output

A 1, 2 and 3 only   B 1, 3 and 5 only   C 1, 5 and 6 only
D 1, 3, 5 and 6 only   E 3, 4, 5 and 6 only

Questions 300–302 refer to the following instruments of economic policy:

1 Tighter HP restrictions
2 Lower interest rates
3 A call for special deposits
4 Increased government spending
5 Increased taxation
6 Increased welfare benefits
7 The sale of securities on the open market by the Bank of England's broker
8 Increased investment grants

300 Which of these measures are classified as monetary policy?

A 2 and 7 only   B 1, 2 and 7 only   C 3, 7 and 8 only
D 1, 2, 3 and 7 only   E 1, 2, 3, 6 and 8 only

301 Which of the measures are classified as fiscal policy?

A 4, 5 and 6 only   B 1, 2, 4 and 5 only   C 3, 4, 5 and 6 only
D 4, 5, 6 and 8 only   E 1, 2, 3, 6 and 8 only

302 Which of the measures would probably form part of a deflationary package?

A 1 and 5 only   B 1, 3 and 5 only   C 1, 4 and 7 only
D 1, 2, 3 and 5 only   E 1, 3, 5 and 7 only

303 If the government's aim is to reduce total domestic purchasing power it will most probably

A pursue a policy of cheap money and aim at a budget surplus
B aim at a budget deficit and operate a credit squeeze
C plan a budget surplus and operate a tight money policy
D plan a budget deficit and operate a cheap money policy
E use a system of price controls and rationing

304 Which of the following conditions would tend to make reduced tariff a suitable remedy for domestic, demand–pull, inflation?

1 The country has a large balance of payments surplus
2 There is a high propensity to import.
3 The supply of imports is elastic.

A 1, 2 and 3   B 1 and 2 only   C 2 and 3 only
D 1 only   E 3 only

5 The effectiveness of monetary policy in a depression will be reduced if

A the central bank is reluctant to allow the price of government securities to fall
B the central bank is committed to an 'easy money' policy
C liquidity preference is relatively low
D the demand for money as an asset is very strong

6 Taking into account the other objectives of government economic policy, which of the following measures would be most appropriate for dealing with *frictional* unemployment?

1 An expansion of the facilities for industrial retraining
2 The provision of generous redundancy payments
3 An expansion of aggregate demand

A 1, 2 and 3
B 1 and 2 only
C 2 and 3 only
D 1 only
E 3 only

Questions 307 and 308 are based on the following information:

In an economy the current level of national income is £10,000 million. The full employment level of income is estimated to be £12,000 million. In this economy any rise in total final expenditure which creates additional income of £100 will, through its effects on income and consumption, create eventually a secondary increase of income equal to £33$\frac{1}{3}$.

7 What is the value of the multiplier?

A $\frac{1}{3}$
B 1½
C 3
D Cannot be determined from the information given.

308 Assuming no change in the other propensities to spend and save, and no change in the rates of taxation, by how much must the level of government expenditure on goods and services be increased in order t achieve full employment?

A £666²⁄₃m

B £1,333¹⁄₃m

C £2,000m

D £6,000m

309 The question is based on the following quotation:

'Public spending is expected to be about £32,000 million this year. About 60% of this is spent on goods and services and 40% is paid to people in benefits, grants and subsidies.'

On the basis of this information it can be said that public spending as a component of aggregate demand amounts to

A £12,800m

B £19,200m

C £32,000m

D £32,000m × the multiplier

310 The Phillips curve seemed to indicate that the government was faced with a choice between two of the following objectives. Which two?

1 Inflation
2 Full employment
3 A balance of payments' surplus
4 A high rate of growth

    A 1 and 2
    B 1 and 3
    C 2 and 3
    D 2 and 4
    E 1 and 4